BEN & JERRY

ICE CREAM FOR EVERYONE!

BY

Keith Elliot Greenberg

Illustrations by Dave Kilmer

A BLACKBIRCH PRESS BOOK

WOODBRIDGE, CONNECTICUT

Published by Blackbirch Press, Inc.
One Bradley Road
Woodbridge , CT 06525

©1994 Blackbirch Press, Inc.
First Edition

Printed in Hong Kong

10 9 8 7 6 5 4 3 2 1

Author and Publisher's Note
The author and publisher wish to thank Lee Holden, Rob Michalak, and Mitch Curren from Ben & Jerry's public relations department for all their valuable help in putting this book together. Information came from the company's promotional material and 1991 Annual Report, as well as *Ben & Jerry's Ice Cream and Dessert Book*, published by Workman Publishing in 1987, and articles from the following publications: *USA Weekend, People, Business Ethics, Harrowsmith, The Wall Street Journal, MPR Exchange, The New Yorker, Inc., Rolling Stone* and *Newsday*.

Library of Congress Cataloging-in-Publication Data

Greenberg, Keith Elliot.
    Ben & Jerry: ice cream for everyone! / by Keith Elliot Greenberg. —
1st ed.
       p.   cm. — (Partners)
    Includes index.
    ISBN 1-56711-064-9 ISBN 1-56711-068-1 (Pbk.)
    1. Ben & Jerry's (Firm)—History—Juvenile literature. 2. Cohen, Ben
(Ben R.)—Juvenile literature. 3. Greenfield, Jerry—Juvenile literature. 4. Ben &
Jerry's (Firm) 5. Businessmen—United States—Biography—Juvenile literature.
6. Ice cream industry—United States—History—Juvenile literature. [1. Cohen,
Ben (Ben R.) 2. Greenfield, Jerry. 3. Ben & Jerry's (Firm) 4. Businessmen.
5. Ice cream industry.] I. Title. II. Title: Ben and Jerry. III. Series.
HD9281.U54B464 1994
338.7'6374—dc20   93-42742
                                                 CIP
                                                 AC

••• Contents •••

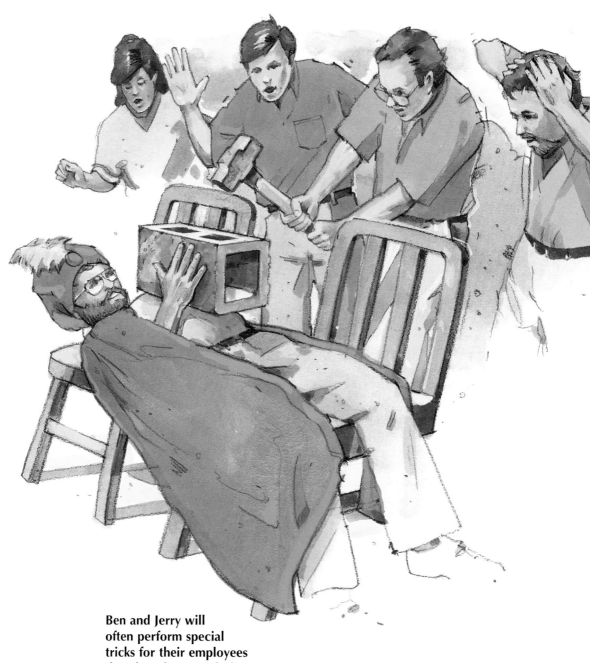

Ben and Jerry will
often perform special
tricks for their employees
that show how much the two
partners really trust each other.

• •• | •••

A Flavorful Combination

In most companies, the bosses don't behave like this. Ben Cohen has been known to dress up like an old snake charmer from India at employee parties, with his large belly puffing out from the bottom of a small shirt. He will lay across two chairs as a cinderblock is placed on his stomach. Because his belly is so big, sometimes the cinderblock rolls off. Then someone has to put it on his stomach again.

Next, Jerry Greenfield appears, holding a sledge-hammer—Jerry is Ben's partner in Ben & Jerry's ice cream company. As music plays, Jerry thrusts back the heavy weapon and smashes the cinderblock to pieces—without injuring Ben.

5

Jerry learned this trick when he took a class in carnival skills during college. But the purpose of this kind of stunt is also to teach a lesson. Ben and Jerry are a team. And they want people to know that they trust each other. When Ben shows he isn't afraid of Jerry's mighty hammer, that's trust.

Ben and Jerry both believe a company doesn't have to be stuffy to be successful. In fact, they say that people work better when they're having fun on the job. At the company's employee parties, there have been hula-hoop competitions, yo-yo shows, and Ben-and-Jerry-lookalike contests. Jerry has used his carnival lessons to swallow fire, and has even allowed workers to dunk him in a water tank.

A Sense of Humor

If anything, Ben & Jerry's is a company with a sense of humor. Instead of handsome models on their ice cream containers, Ben and Jerry have a picture of themselves eating ice cream. The two have traveled around America in a camper called the "Cowmobile." From the camper, Ben and Jerry serve free scoops to customers. Even their flavors have funny names, such as "Chunky Monkey" and "Cherry Garcia" (named after Jerry Garcia, the singer of a popular rock group). In 1987, when the American economy seemed to be in trouble, they even created a flavor called "Economic Crunch."

In a report to the company's investors, Ben repeated a comment made by a man called Wavy Gravy. Wavy Gravy was the master of ceremonies at a famous music festival held in Woodstock, New York, in the 1960s. Wavy Gravy said, "We are all the same person trying to shake hands with ourselves." What does this mean? It means all people are partners on the same planet, so they should join hands and cooperate. Ben and Jerry remembered this statement and liked it so much they named one of their newest flavors "Wavy Gravy."

They also try to live by Wavy Gravy's words, making great efforts to improve the world.

Making the World a Better Place

Workers at Ben & Jerry's three ice cream factories in Vermont are encouraged to devote free time to positive causes. When employees were questioned about the things they cared about, most said they wanted to help children. As a result, the company

began giving more money to organizations that aided youngsters.

The company donates 7.5 percent of its profits to community groups, much more than most American corporations. Ben and Jerry also started a Ben & Jerry's Foundation to assist groups dedicated to cleaning up the environment, teaching people job skills, and treating drug-addicted mothers.

Throughout history, women have not had the same job opportunities as men. Because of this, Ben

Ben and Jerry have traveled the country in their "Cowmobile," handing out free scoops of ice cream and spreading the word about their company.

& Jerry's goes out of its way to make sure that qualified women are recognized. As of 1992, half the people in charge of the company's different departments were women.

"To me, the business sort of exists not really to make ice cream or to make money, but...to bring joy into the world," Jerry says. Ben agrees, and adds that the purpose is making the world "more just and fair. So together, we have this vision of doing great things in a fun way."

9

Success Along with Fun

Although they've had tough times like every other company, Ben and Jerry's attitude has brought them good fortune. Except for Haagen-Dazs, Ben & Jerry's sells the most "superpremium" ("gourmet") ice cream in supermarkets. And sales go up every year.

"Our biggest argument ever was about ice cream chunk size," *Jerry recalls.*

Despite the difficulty of owning and running a large company, Ben Cohen and Jerry Greenfield always remember that, before their fame, they were good friends. To this day, that friendship remains solid. As Jerry recalls, "Our biggest argument ever was about ice cream chunk size." Both Ben and Jerry realize that their deep friendship is one of the most basic keys to their success. If they hadn't been able to work so well together, their company would probably never have made it. But their friendship did not happen overnight. It goes back to a time when they were both in seventh grade in a small town on Long Island, New York.

••• 2 •••

The Early Years

Ben Cohen and Jerry Greenfield grew up a mile and a half apart in Merrick, New York. The town, known for its green lawns and comfortable homes, is located on Long Island. Most of Merrick's residents were New York City professionals—Jerry's father was a stockbroker, Ben's was an accountant.

The First Meeting

The boys had never met each other until 1963, when they were placed in the same seventh grade gym class at Merrick Avenue Junior High School. Neither was a great athlete. "We were the two slowest, chubbiest guys in the seventh grade," Jerry remembers. "We were nerds."

It was an autumn day when coach Robert Phelps asked the class to run a mile around the track. A few minutes later, most of the boys were headed to the finish line, but Ben and Jerry were far behind.

The coach tried to get them to run faster. "Gentlemen," he shouted at the two boys, "if you don't run the mile in under seven minutes, you're going to have to do it again!"

Jerry wanted to speed up, but Ben decided to argue. "Gee coach," he said, "if I don't do it under seven minutes the first time, I'm *certainly* not going to do it under seven minutes the second time."

Ben and Jerry were often scolded by their gym teacher for being two of the slowest kids in the class.

Ben's reasoning made perfect sense to Jerry. After all, how could they run faster a second time if they were already so tired? Jerry decided right then and there that he wanted to become Ben's friend. "This was a guy I wanted to know," Jerry says. "This was a real *thinker*."

Ben and Jerry both had to be thinkers, because people didn't accept them based on their looks or abilities on the athletic field. Generally, they attracted friends because they knew how to make people laugh. Years later, they'd use that humor to inspire customers to buy Ben & Jerry's ice cream.

High School Years

While attending Merrick's Sanford H. Calhoun High School, the friends spent weekends going to square dances at nearby Jones Beach. "That's the type of kids we were," Jerry says. "We didn't drink beer, we went square dancing at Jones Beach. A whole bunch of us guys would find girls and ask them to square dance, and that was a big night for us."

As kids, Ben and Jerry went to square dances on the weekends.

Of the two, Jerry was considered the better student. He graduated third in his class, and friends suggested he become a doctor. "I think I was pushed towards thinking about being a doctor because I was good at math and science," he says. Although he was a big sports fan, he added, "I wasn't good enough at sports to play them."

Ben was more of a rebel. He became enraged that there were no doors on the toilet stalls at the high school, and started a campaign to get some installed. He wrote an essay about the situation and brought it to the school newspaper. "It was called WSSIP," Ben recalls, "We Shall Sit In Peace. They wouldn't print it."

A Brief Partnership

Ben's start in the ice cream business came during one summer vacation. That's when he began driving an ice cream truck through Merrick, earning $100 a week and all the free ice cream he wanted. Ben talked Jerry into driving another truck, but Jerry quit after a week. Although it didn't last long, this was the very first Ben and Jerry partnership.

After graduation, Jerry went to Oberlin College in Ohio to prepare for his medical studies. Ben went to Colgate University in upstate New York. After a year, he dropped out and traveled around the country, stopping off in Ohio to visit his friend.

Next, Ben enrolled in Skidmore College in the town of Saratoga, New York. There, he studied pottery and jewelry-making. After awhile, he dropped out again, and took a number of odd jobs. He drove a taxi and worked in a bakery kitchen. When he was hired as a security guard at the horse racing track in Saratoga, he wore a holster, but no gun. "None of these jobs ever lasted more than a few months," he says. "Finally, I ended up in a small town in upstate New York called Paradox, working with emotionally disturbed children."

Meanwhile, Jerry graduated from Oberlin. He planned to attend medical school, so he could become a doctor. But he could not find a school that would accept him.

Getting Together

"By this time, we both realized we weren't really getting where we wanted to go," Ben recalls. "So we decided to change our courses and head there together. We weren't interested in making a lot of money. We just wanted to do something. . .fun."

Ben and Jerry's very first partnership involved selling ice cream.

At first, their career plans had nothing to do with ice cream. Ben and Jerry wanted to start a bagel business. Their idea was to copy United Parcel Service, or U.P.S., which delivers packages to homes and offices. Ben and Jerry would bring bagels to people's homes, and call their company U.B.S.—for United Bagel Service.

But after one phone call about the price of a bagel machine, Ben and Jerry were disappointed. Bagel equipment was too expensive, so they chose to go into the ice cream trade instead.

Sweet Success

Ben and Jerry have often been asked why they picked the ice cream profession. Both joke that their choice had something to do with their healthy appetites. "We were both big into eating," Jerry says. "And I think ice cream was just among the things we ate."

During the 1960s, Ben and Jerry were what many people called long-haired *"hippies"* who believed that people should concentrate more on promoting peace than making money. "We grew up . . . when it wasn't cool to be businessmen," Jerry explains. Their goal was to make their customers happy, rather than simply to become rich. So they vowed to create great ice cream flavors, and open a store where everyone felt at home.

17

The First Store

In 1977, they found an abandoned gas station in Burlington, Vermont. Ben remembers entering the building for the first time. It was "falling apart," he recalls. "You could see daylight through the roof. There were six inches of ice on the floor, hardly any walls, no ceiling and whatever was left standing was badly water damaged."

Still, they liked the location, so they borrowed money to fix up the place. Jerry contributed $4,000, Ben $2,000, and Ben's father another $2,000. The partners also received a $4,000 loan from the bank. Ben and Jerry's friends helped them build new walls, repair the ceiling and install new electrical wires and pipes. The pair held a "painting party" to decorate the store white and orange. When they were done, they had a second painting party because they decided they didn't like orange after all.

Cooperation and Compromise

They spoke about whether they should call their store Ben & Jerry's or Jerry & Ben's. It was agreed that Ben & Jerry's sounded better. But because Ben's name came first, Jerry was named president of the

Before they opened their first store, Ben and Jerry worked hard together to master the skills of ice-cream-making.

business and Ben the vice-president. This kind of *compromise* and fairness has always been a key to their successful partnership.

In order to master their craft, they bought a large book called *Ice Cream*, which explained how to make many flavors. They also purchased a very old ice-cream-maker and started experimenting. Not everything they made was perfect. "I once made a batch of 'Rum Raisin' that stretched and bounced," Jerry remembers with a smile.

Then, they found out about an ice cream class that Pennsylvania State University was offering by

19

mail. The lessons only cost $5.00, so the partners contributed $2.50 a piece. "We bought fresh cream, milk and eggs, and bags of *rock salt* for the ice cream maker," Ben says. "We chopped the ice right out of the lake. Every day, we studied our lessons." After 14 weeks of studying, the two finally felt ready to invite customers to sample their cones.

A Grand Opening

The store officially opened on May 5, 1978. Jerry was in charge of ice-cream-making and Ben made hot food. Their friend, Don Rose, volunteered to entertain customers by playing the piano. The partners were so grateful to him that they named him a "Ben & Jerry's lifer." For the rest of his life, Don Rose can get Ben & Jerry's ice cream for free.

Word of a great new ice cream company spread quickly through Vermont.

For every season, Ben and Jerry created a different way to bring customers to their store. During the summer, they showed free movies on the wall of the building next door. During the coldest winter days, they offered a penny off for every celsius degree below zero. Later, they created a "Lick Winter " contest. The contestants actually got to eat dinner with Jerry's parents, and spend a day at Disney World with Ben's uncle.

At first, Ben and Jerry only expected to serve 100 customers a day. But soon they were scooping cones for ten times as many people. After running out of their best flavors, they'd sell what Ben called their "weirdest and least delicious flavor experiments." But even those sold out.

The Word Spreads

Word about the ice cream parlor spread around Burlington. The owner of a downtown restaurant asked for permission to sell Ben & Jerry's ice cream, too. This gave the partners an idea. Why not pack their ice cream into containers and start distributing it all over Vermont?

Ben agreed to travel around the state, selling to the different stores while Jerry stayed in Burlington and supervised the ice-cream-making. Two years after their start, the pair opened a factory in an old spool-and-bobbin mill. "Things were great," Ben remembers. "Twelve people were working for us downtown. Jerry was coming up with ever stranger flavors, and I had become a traveling salesman."

In 1983, the people of Ben & Jerry's created the world's largest ice cream sundae. It weighed 27,102 pounds and was covered with 1,400 pounds of maple syrup.

Success was coming more quickly than anyone had expected. Ben & Jerry's opened a second ice cream store in Shelburne, Vermont, and their flavors were now available in supermarkets. *Time* magazine called Ben & Jerry's "the best ice cream in the world." By 1983, the company was selling over a million dollars in ice cream a year.

And Ben and Jerry knew how to keep people talking about them. Newspapers and magazines all over the world wrote about their construction of the world's largest ice cream sundae. The partners qualified for the *Guinness Book of World Records* by building the sundae in St. Albans, Vermont, that weighed 27,102 pounds. Over 20,400 pounds of ice cream were used, along with 2,000 pounds of sliced pineapples and 1,400 pounds of maple syrup.

As the company grew, Ben and Jerry had a hard time keeping up with business demands. One day, they had to shut their business and put up a sign that read, "WE'RE CLOSED BECAUSE WE'RE TRYING TO FIGURE OUT WHAT'S GOING ON." They even considered selling the company. But then they decided to keep it, remembering their dream of using their company's wealth to help the world.

··· **4** ···

How Big Is Too Big?

By the early 1980s, the old gas station that had served as Ben & Jerry's first store was long closed. Jerry had gained about 40 pounds from testing and eating ice cream, and his girlfriend said she wanted to attend graduate school in Arizona. After thinking it over, he decided to go with her. For a while, Ben and Jerry's partnership would be a long-distance one.

The company "was too big for me," Jerry recalls. "I was more comfortable in the filling station."

In Arizona, Jerry volunteered at the public library. But he still owned part of the business, and spoke to Ben often. They mostly talked about the threat being posed by their main *rival,* Haagen-Dazs.

25

Scooping the Competition

For several years, Haagen-Dazs had not had much competition. Now, Ben & Jerry's was appearing in the same stores, and taking away customers. Both brands of ice cream were often brought to groceries by the same distributors, but Haagen-Dazs now pledged not to do business with the distributors who continued to work with Ben & Jerry's.

The partners decided to make the public aware of their battle. They noted that Haagen-Dazs was actually owned by a larger company, Pillsbury. Most Americans had watched Pillsbury's television ads, and were familiar with the Pillsbury Doughboy—a character on commercials who was supposed to be made out of dough. Ben & Jerry's new slogan became, "What's the Doughboy Afraid Of?" This saying appeared on Ben & Jerry's pints, T-shirts, bumper stickers, and signs on Boston buses. Jerry left Arizona to help the cause. He arrived in front of Pillsbury headquarters in Minneapolis one day, looking tanned and slimmer than before. For a week, he stood outside the building, wearing a sign asking, "What's the Doughboy Afraid Of?" Even the Pillsbury workers admired his determination.

When Haagen-Dazs threatened
Ben and Jerry's distribution, the
two partners started a public
campaign to battle their giant
competitor.

Eventually, both sides made peace. Haagen-Dazs took back its warning to distributors. Ben & Jerry's would still be available everywhere.

A New Plant

Shortly afterwards, Jerry returned to Vermont. Plans were underway to move from Burlington to the town of Waterbury, 30 miles away. One of Ben & Jerry's

most valuable workers, Fred "Chico" Lager, traveled around the state to raise money for the new plant. He made Vermont residents a special *stock offering* and persuaded them by offering them a taste of Ben & Jerry's ice cream.

Demand for Ben & Jerry's ice cream continued to increase. By 1988, employees had to work 12 hours a day just to make enough ice cream to satisfy the

By 1988, Ben and Jerry's employees had to work 12 hours a day just to keep up with the customer demand for their ice cream.

demand. When more orders came in, even the managers and office workers put on factory uniforms and worked. Finally, a second factory was opened in Springfield, Vermont.

Helping Springfield

Ben and Jerry chose Springfield because many people there were out of work and the ice cream plant provided badly needed jobs. During slow periods, some Ben & Jerry's employees were kept busy by

When production slowed down at the Springfield, Vermont, plant, some employees would do work in the community instead.

doing community work in town. Every Saturday during the summer, people came to the plant to watch free movies—and eat free ice cream.

Caring About Employees

Ben and Jerry believe that it is important for their employees to think of themselves as part of a family. They had a survey taken to find out the likes and dislikes of their workers, and the partners paid close attention to the answers. The more positive the workers felt about their company, the more care they would put into the product.

A decision was also made to slow down the ice-cream-making pace for several months. Demand for Ben & Jerry's was still high, but the partners wanted to be best prepared to meet that demand. To Ben, the growing popularity of his product was like a giant wave of ice cream. "We were all trying to stay in front of this wave so we could keep on getting carried along by it," he said. "And we were all going crazy. And I said maybe it's time for us to stop trying to keep up with the wave, and take our time and build a boat. Once we had that boat built, we could go anywhere we wanted."

··· 5 ···

A Happy and Helpful Workplace

One of Ben and Jerry's greatest fears was that, as the company got bigger, it would be less fun to work there. In 1988, Jerry approached a group of employees and asked them if they'd like to join his "Joy Gang." Their job would be "bringing joy and laughter" to others at Ben & Jerry's.

Many people stepped forward and volunteered for the Joy Gang. As a start, Jerry appointed himself "Minister of Joy."

The Joy Gang held dinners for employees of certain departments simply to put them in a good mood. The group also organized an Elvis Presley Appreciation Day. Workers were asked to show up on the job dressed like the flashy rock'n'roll singer. At the Joy Gang's "Scurvy Derby," employees raced their favorite toy cars down a stairwell. The high-light of one Halloween party was watching one of the company's bosses—six-foot-seven-inch, 220-pound Chuck Lacey—dance across the front patio in a pink ballet dress.

Joy Gang member Sean Greenwood says the group proves that Ben & Jerry's is "a place where people can be themselves and be accepted for that.... Ben & Jerry's is a place where you can work and feel good about the results."

Caring for Children and Workers

Ben & Jerry's also takes extra care of its employees. They vote on which charities the company will fund. There's a health club and day-care center, and work-ers may receive money for college from the company. Plus, everyone is allowed to take home three free pints of ice cream a day!

Children are one of the company's most impor-tant concerns. Ben & Jerry's is one of the few American companies that allows fathers to take off for two weeks—with full pay—after their wives give birth. Anyone adopting a child is allowed between two and four paid weeks at home.

Jerry's "Joy Gang" organized an "Elvis Appreciation Day" when everyone was asked to dress up like the famous rock 'n' roll singer.

No matter how well Ben & Jerry's ice cream sells, executives are limited to humble salaries. Even the top bosses are not allowed to make more than seven times as much as the lowest-paid worker. By comparison, the top executives at most American corporations earn well over 90 times as much as the average factory employee.

Retreats are held so workers can better know one another. People will often play a game where they will climb a ladder and then fall backwards—into the arms of fellow employees. The purpose of this game is to teach trust. Workers also gather in small groups to talk over and share personal issues.

Whatever it takes, Ben and Jerry want employees to know that they're important. "The focus isn't Ben and Jerry anymore," Jerry says. "The focus is 500 people. This isn't a story about two former hippies. It's about a whole new kind of company."

Helping the Planet

For some reason, people in the ice cream business have always been concerned about the well-being of others. America's first big ice-cream-maker was Jacob Fussell, a milk dealer from Baltimore who

At company retreats, employees have a chance to participate in activities that build trust and friendship for all.

began producing the frozen dessert in 1851. Aside from being a businessman, Fussell was a religious Quaker who fought hard to end slavery in the United States.

Ben and Jerry have also put a great deal of effort into correcting the wrongs around them. Among the most disturbing things the partners noticed was the way people treat the environment. In a typical office, people throw out paper cups and boxes without thinking. In time, this garbage just sits in large dumps or gets discarded in the ocean. Ben and Jerry wanted their company to do something about this problem, so they created a recycling program.

Stationery, computer paper, cardboard, plastic, and even greeting cards are collected at Ben & Jerry's factories and scoop shops. These items are then sent to recycling plants to be used again. The company has also set a formal policy for conserving paper and other products made from natural resources. Whenever possible, employees are encouraged to use both sides of a piece of paper. And all the company's reports and brochures are printed on recycled paper.

In 1991, Ben & Jerry's sent a group of entertainers on a tour bus across the United States to put on a circus-like show in different communities. Performers would sing and tell jokes, while workers gave away ice cream. But there was more to this event than simply teaching people that Ben & Jerry's is a fun company. The bus's freezers, sound system, and lights were all powered by solar energy. And during and after the show, members of the audience received information about how each of them could chip in and do their part to protect the environment.

Ben and Jerry's company has worked hard to protect the environment.

Working to Help Those in Need

The wrappers of Ben & Jerry's Peace Pops ice cream bars tell about another cause important to the founders: *poverty* in America. As a customer munches on the snack, he or she can read about ways to help children in need of food and education.

For many years, Ben & Jerry's has bought its milk from family farms in Vermont. In 1991, the price of milk suddenly went down around the country, and farmers were in serious trouble. But Ben and Jerry announced that their company would still pay the same prices for milk as before. Family farms were important, they said, and they would help them stay in business. The company even set up a special telephone number so customers could call and find out how they could help family farms.

Helping Others Help Themselves

There have been other efforts made to do business with the disadvantaged. Because black farmers have traditionally been poorer than white farmers, the company buys peaches and pecans from minorities. Ben & Jerry's "Wild Maine Blueberry" ice cream is made entirely from berries that are harvested by

Maine's Passamaquoddy Indians. The brownies in the "Chocolate Fudge Brownie" flavor are made by homeless people.

In July 1991, a New York lawyer named Joe Holland hired 12 homeless people to work at his new Ben & Jerry's ice cream parlor in Harlem. Most of the people he hired had lost their homes because of drugs. Now, they were drug free, and hoping to

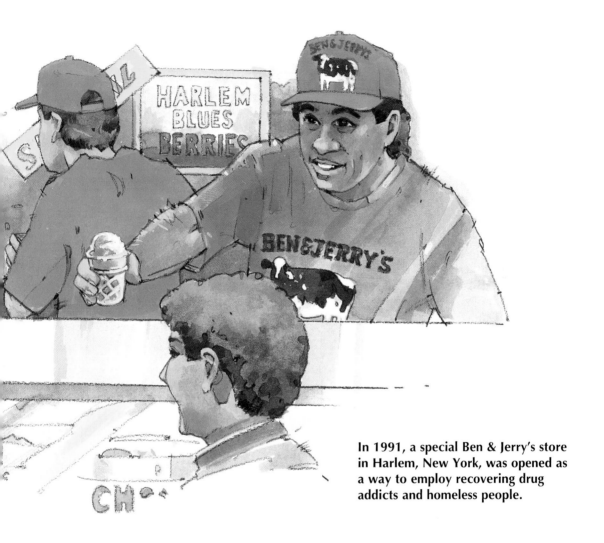

In 1991, a special Ben & Jerry's store in Harlem, New York, was opened as a way to employ recovering drug addicts and homeless people.

get a fresh start. Because Holland was working for such a good cause, Ben and Jerry allowed him to open the store without any fee.

The first week, 4,500 customers passed through the store. Ben and Jerry also allowed the store to have its own special flavor. Raspberry ice cream was mixed with blueberry swirl and chunks of straw-berry to create "Harlem Blues Berries."

41

••• 6 •••

Teaming for Tomorrow

en & Jerry's past is both funny and fascinating. But the founders realize that it is now more important to look ahead than look back.

"You don't want to stay stuck in the past," Jerry says. "The gas station we started in was an amazing place, but it is there no longer. It's a parking lot. You can tell wonderful stories about the place—but tell me the wonderful story about what happened at the plant last month." Looking ahead, Jerry says, "I think our company will be changed. I think there's no doubt about that. . . . We just have to make it a good change."

Flexibility between the partners has helped keep the company's changes positive. In the early 1980s, when Jerry moved to Arizona, Ben was happy to run the company from Vermont. In 1992, it was Jerry's turn to oversee the business while Ben was away. For six months, Ben took time off to study *welding,* a hobby he's always enjoyed.

Although they've developed a successful formula for selling ice cream and addressing social issues, Ben and Jerry continue to experiment.

In 1990, they introduced a low fat ice cream called "Ben & Jerry's Light." This was after President George Bush said that any American who performed outstanding acts was one of "1,000 points of light." Ben and Jerry placed their own twist on the statement with a "1,000 Pints of Light" campaign. Special people who helped their communities were awarded 1,000 pints of "Light" ice cream.

Unfortunately, customers were not as interested in the light product as Ben and Jerry hoped. Sales were low, and Ben & Jerry's stopped making it.

"We're learning as we go," Jerry says. "I mean, there aren't any blueprints for doing this. It's to be expected that you'll make mistakes when you're breaking new ground."

Still for every error, there are many pluses. "Chocolate Chip Cookie Dough" was introduced in

1991, and quickly became the company's best seller. "It's been a fabulous flavor for us," says Ben & Jerry's chief financial officer Frances Rathke. "It grabbed a lot of people's attention. It's one of the things we'll have in our history book."

A year later, the company came out with very popular frozen yogurt in well-known Ben & Jerry's flavors like "Cherry Garcia" and "Heath Bar

Ben and Jerry are proud of the success they have achieved together. As they had hoped, their company has not only made great ice cream, it has also made the world a better place.

Crunch." A reporter for a newsletter covering the ice cream business observed that Ben and Jerry "continue to find something new to offer that refreshes everyone's appetite."

What's Next?

To keep up with demand for their ice cream, a third factory in St. Albans, Vermont, was opened in 1994. Meanwhile, customers keep trying to guess which new flavors the company will create. A 1992 article in *The Wall Street Journal* mentioned "Sweet Potato Pie" and "Tropical Fruit" as possibilities.

As for Ben and Jerry—the two slowest, heaviest kids in seventh grade—their achievements seem like something out of a movie. "I would say it's all quite a shock to us," Jerry admits. "And quite frankly, it's a shock to anyone who knows us." But Ben and Jerry have always had a strong friendship and have always worked well with each other. Although they each have different talents and personalities, they share many important goals and dreams. Working together, they have been able to make many of those dreams come true for themselves and for many other people in the world.

Glossary

compromise Coming to an agreement by blending your wishes with someone else's.

contestant A person who participates in a contest or competition.

hippies A term from the 1960s that was used to describe young, long-haired, rebellious people.

poverty The state of being extremely poor.

rival Competitor.

rock salt Special, large-grained salt used to chill down cream during the ice-cream-making process.

stock offering An opportunity to put money into a company and share in its profits.

welding A metalworking craft.

Further Reading

Cobb, Vicki. *The Scoop on Ice Cream.* New York: Little, Brown & Company, 1985.

Jaspersohn, William. *Ice Cream.* New York: Macmillan, 1988.

Keller, Stella. *Ice Cream.* Madison, New Jersey: Raintree Steck-Vaughn, 1989.

Neimark, Jill. *Ice Cream.* Mamaroneck, New York: Hastings House, 1986.

Olders, Jules. *Ben & Jerry...The Real Scoop!* Shelburne, Vermont: Chapters, 1993.

Willard, Dennis. *The Incredible Ice Cream Book.* Pinellas Park, Florida: Willowisp Press, 1987.

Index